APPETITE for life!

FLORA

Getting Britain's Heart in Training

CONTENTS

Flora is a registered trademark

Design © Arcturus Publishing
Limited 2002
Recipes © Antony Worrall
Thompson 2002

ISBN 1-84193-107-1

Arcturus Publishing Limited
1–7 Shand Street, London SE1 2ES

Food photography by Steve Lee

Antony Worall Thompson
photographed by Hamish Mitchell

Design by Alex Ingr

Cover design © 2002 by Triangle
Communcations Ltd

Printed and bound in Italy

PREFACE

*W*hen a man of my size undertakes the **Flora London Marathon** he has to take it seriously. The only way I was able to complete it was by improving the food I ate, reducing saturated fat and constantly monitoring my heart rate while I trained. **Flora** played an important role in my new regime. Now that I have completed that challenge of a lifetime, I still continue to maintain a healthy diet. They say 'you are what you eat' and I genuinely believe that.

These special recipes form part of my new healthier way of eating. I hope you give them a go. You don't need to be about to run a marathon to justify adopting sensible eating habits. But if you are in training – eat well, believe in yourself and have fun!

Antony Worrall Thompson
MOGB

FOREWORD

*T*he heart is the most important muscle in your body and deserves looking after. The more you do to care for your heart, the healthier and happier your life is likely to be – and being healthy and happy is what this book is all about.

Self-help remains the key to heart health. Eating a healthy diet that includes plenty of fruit and vegetables is important for us all. Cutting back on fat in general, and switching from saturated fats like butter and lard, to polyunsaturated types, such as margarines and spreads and vegetable oils, will help maintain a healthy heart. And, as this collection of Antony Worrall Thompson's tempting recipes proves, eating healthily doesn't mean you have to sacrifice flavour and enjoyment.

The heart thrives on being put to full use and years of research have shown that people who exercise regularly lead longer and healthier lives.

Two years ago Antony Worrall Thompson would have been the first to admit that his waistline and athletic prowess left much to be desired, but after an intensive training programme he completed the **Flora London Marathon**. It's amazing what you can achieve if you try, as Charlie Dimmock is about to find out, along with the forty other novices who make up *Team Flora*.

If Antony and Charlie can do it – so can you! Any improvement in your diet and lifestyle is a step in the right direction – and all journeys, however long, must start with a single step.

Dr Mark Porter

HERBED TOMATO PASTA

Servings: 4

Preparation time
15 minutes

Cooking time
8–10 minutes

INGREDIENTS

- 3 garlic cloves, finely chopped
- 3 spring onions, finely sliced
- 55g (2oz) pine nuts, toasted and coarsely chopped
- 4 large tomatoes, roughly chopped
- 3 tbsp shredded mint leaves
- 3 tbsp shredded rocket
- 3 tbsp chopped flat-leaf parsley
- 3 tbsp **Flora Oil**
- 1 tbsp lemon juice
- ground black pepper
- 350–450g (¾–1lb) spaghetti

A very quick recipe with fresh, vibrant flavours. The only cooking required is of the pasta, the heat from which will gently wilt the rocket and herbs. You could add other ingredients for variety, such as flakes of canned tuna or chopped lean ham.

Combine all the ingredients except the pasta in a bowl and season to taste.

Cook the pasta in plenty of boiling water, following packet instruction, until just cooked (*al dente*).

Drain the pasta well and toss with the raw sauce until the herbs start to wilt. Serve immediately.

ORIENTAL PRAWN AND NOODLE SALAD

Servings: 4–6

Preparation time
10 minutes

Cooking time
1 minute

INGREDIENTS

• 225g (8oz) sugar snap peas • 1 tbsp **Flora Oil**
1 tsp sesame oil • 2 tbsp rice vinegar • 3 tbsp light soy sauce • 1 garlic clove, crushed • 1 fresh red chilli, finely chopped or ½ tsp chilli paste • 1 tbsp finely chopped fresh coriander • 280g (10oz) cooked peeled prawns • 3 spring onions, finely sliced • 450g (1lb) cooked soba or egg noodles • 1 tbsp toasted sesame seeds

This is a great lunch dish, quick to make and full of oriental flavours. If you don't have rice vinegar in the store cupboard, white wine or sherry vinegar could be used as a substitute.

Cook the sugar snap peas in a large pan of boiling water for 1 minute. Drain and refresh under cold water.

In a large bowl, combine the oils, vinegar, soy sauce, garlic, chilli and coriander. Add the cooked prawns and toss to combine. Add the peas, spring onions and noodles and toss everything together.

Transfer to a serving bowl and sprinkle with the sesame seeds.

CHICKEN PURI SANDWICH

Servings: 4

Preparation time
20 minutes

Cooking time
20 minutes

INGREDIENTS

• 1 tbsp **Flora Oil** • 1 tsp
five-spice powder • 1 red
onion, finely chopped
• 3 boneless chicken
breasts, skinned and cut
into thin strips of 1cm
• 2.5cm (1in) cube of
fresh root ginger, peeled
and grated • 2–3 large
garlic cloves, crushed
• ½ tsp chilli powder,
or to taste • 1 tsp garam
masala • 2 tsp tomato
purée • 1 tbsp lemon juice
• 2 tbsp finely chopped
fresh coriander

To serve: mini wholemeal
pitta breads, warmed

*The secret to this dish is the blend of
spices, which also works very well with
prawns. The dish is quite hot and spicy,
so remember the chilli is optional.*

Heat the **Flora Oil** in a small saucepan, add
the five-spice powder and allow to sizzle
gently for 30–40 seconds. Add the onion
and cook, stirring frequently, for about 5
minutes until soft.

Add the chicken and cook for 10
minutes, stirring occasionally, until golden-
brown and cooked through – do not
overcook. Stir in the ginger, garlic, chilli and
garam masala and cook for 1–2 minutes.
Add the tomato purée, lemon juice and
coriander, stirring well until combined.

Spoon the mixture into warmed, split
pitta breads and serve with lettuce, onion,
tomatoes, coriander, a drizzle of yoghurt
and lime wedges.

PUMPKIN AND BUTTER BEAN SOUP

Servings: 6

Preparation time
15 minutes

Cooking time
1 hour

INGREDIENTS

• 900g (2lb) pumpkin or butternut squash, cut into 7.5–10cm (3–4in) chunks and de-seeded
• 2 tbsp **Flora Oil**
• freshly ground black pepper • 1 tsp fresh thyme leaves • 3 whole garlic cloves, peeled
• 1 large onion, finely chopped • 850ml (1½ pt) good vegetable stock
• 2 tbsp tomato purée
• pinch of cayenne pepper
• 400g can butter beans, drained and rinsed

To serve: thyme leaves and wholemeal granary rolls, warmed

This wonderful warming vegetarian soup is colourful and filling. Add canned beans if you want to turn it into a protein dish. Don't worry if you can't get pumpkin – butternut squash works equally well.

Preheat oven to 190°C/375°F/Gas 5. Place the pumpkin or squash in a roasting tin, drizzle with 1 tbsp **Flora Oil**, season with pepper and sprinkle with thyme. Place in the oven and bake for 15 minutes.

Add the garlic cloves and continue to bake for about 25–30 minutes or until the pumpkin or squash is soft. When cool enough to handle, scoop the flesh of the pumpkin or squash from its skin using a spoon. Set aside.

Heat the remaining **Flora Oil** in a large saucepan, add the onion and cook over a medium heat for 6–8 minutes, stirring occasionally, until very soft. Allow to cool.

Put the pumpkin or squash, onion, stock, tomato purée and cayenne into a food processor or blender and process until smooth.

Pour the soup into the large saucepan, add the butter beans and warm through.

Ladle into warm bowls, garnish with thyme leaves and serve with warmed wholemeal or granary rolls.

SPINACH, BACON & MUSHROOM SALAD

Servings: 4

Preparation time
15 minutes

Cooking time
8 minutes

INGREDIENTS

Dressing: 1½ tbsp **Flora Oil** • 2 tsp lime juice • 1 tsp sherry or wine vinegar • ½ tsp Tabasco sauce • 1 garlic clove, crushed • 1 tbsp chopped basil • 1 tbsp chopped flat-leaf parsley • 1 tbsp snipped chives • ½ tsp ground black pepper

Salad: 1 head chicory, separated into leaves • 4 handfuls baby spinach • 85g (3oz) button mushrooms, cleaned and sliced • ½ cucumber, peeled, halved, de-seeded and cut into small chunks • ½ red onion, finely diced • 3 rashers dry-cure streaky bacon, excess fat and rind removed, cut into 1cm (½ in) strips

This makes for a good brunch dish. If you are a vegetarian you can simply omit the bacon and replace it with courgettes fried in a little Flora Oil *until golden. Similarly you can use your favourite salad leaves instead of the head of chicory.*

Combine all the dressing ingredients and, if possible, leave at least 30 minutes for flavours to develop. (To make the dressing go a little further you can add 2 tablespoons of water.)

Arrange larger chicory leaves in a star shape in a salad dish. Combine smaller leaves with other salad ingredients, except the bacon, and place in a mixing bowl.

Fry the bacon in a hot non-stick pan and cook until crispy, about 8 minutes. Remove the bacon from the pan and set aside.

Add the dressing to the bacon pan and swirl to combine.

Pour the warm dressing over the combined salad and toss. Arrange the salad on top of the chicory and sprinkle with the crispy bacon. Garnish with lemon wedges. Serve immediately, with crusty bread if liked.

VEGETABLE RISOTTO

Servings: 4–6

Preparation time
30 minutes

Cooking time
1 hour

INGREDIENTS

• 1.4 litres (2 ½pt) chicken stock • 55g (2oz) **Flora Original** • 1 tbsp **Flora Oil**
• 1 onion, finely chopped
• 1 garlic clove, finely chopped
• 1 sprig thyme • 1 bay leaf
• 2 carrots, peeled and diced
• 2 courgettes, peeled and diced • 55g (2oz) French beans, topped, tailed and diced • 55g (2oz) frozen garden peas • 450g (1lb) spinach leaves, washed, drained and roughly chopped
• 350g (12oz) arborio rice
• 125ml (4fl oz) white wine
• 55–85g (2–3oz) finely grated Parmesan cheese
• 1 tbsp mascarpone cheese
• chopped fresh flat-leaf parsley to serve

Any combination of your favourite vegetables can be added to this warming dish, which can be served on its own or with grilled fish of your choice.

Heat the stock in a medium saucepan and keep warm.

Melt the **Flora Original** with the **Flora Oil** in a heavy-based saucepan over a medium heat. Add the onion, garlic, thyme and bay leaf and cook for about 5 minutes until the onions are soft but not browned.

Add the carrots and cook for 2 minutes, then add the courgettes, French beans, peas and spinach. Continue to cook for 1–2 minutes, being careful not to brown the vegetables.

Add the rice and stir until the grains are well coated, about 3–4 minutes. Add the wine and stir until it has been absorbed.

Add the stock a ladle at a time, allowing the rice to absorb the liquid each time before adding the next ladle. Continue like this until the rice is tender but still firm to the bite.

When the rice is ready stir in the finely grated Parmesan cheese and mascarpone cheese. Garnish with chopped parsley and serve immediately.

SALMON TABBOULEH

Servings: 4

Preparation time
20 minutes

Cooking time
8 minutes

INGREDIENTS

• 225g (8oz) bulgar wheat • ground black pepper • ¼ tsp ground cinnamon • ½ tsp ground allspice • juice of 1 lemon • 2 tbsp **Flora Oil** • 2 bunches flat-leaf parsley, chopped • ½ bunch mint, chopped • 6 spring onions, thinly sliced • 3 plum tomatoes, de-seeded and diced • 500g (1lb 2oz) fresh salmon fillet • washed herb leaves to garnish

A good tabbouleh needs lots of herbs. I have added a few spices to liven up this version, and served it with salmon, which is a particularly healthy fish.

Soak the bulgar wheat in boiling water for 20 minutes, drain and squeeze dry. Put in a glass bowl and season with pepper, spices, lemon juice and two-thirds of the **Flora Oil**. Leave to stand for 30 minutes before adding the parsley, mint, spring onions and tomatoes.

Brush the salmon fillet with the remaining **Flora Oil**, season with pepper and grill for 3–4 minutes each side, until cooked through. Allow to cool slightly then remove the skin, flake the flesh and fold into the tabbouleh. Serve garnished with herb leaves.

MEDITERRANEAN FISH STEW

Servings: 4–6

Preparation time
30 minutes

Cooking time
15 minutes

INGREDIENTS

• 1 tbsp **Flora Oil**
• 1 onion, finely chopped
• 2 garlic cloves, finely chopped • 1 tsp fresh thyme leaves • 1 tsp fennel seed • 1 bay leaf
• 850ml (1½ pt) fish stock • 500g (1lb 2oz) mussels, cleaned • 450g (1lb) cod, cut into 2.5cm (1in) pieces • 115g (4oz) raw prawns, shelled
• 12 black olives, halved and pitted • 1 red pepper, grilled until skin blackened
• 150ml (¼ pt) passata (sieved tomatoes)
• ½ tsp chopped chillies
• handful of washed fresh basil leaves, torn • ground black pepper

You can add your own favourite fish to this stew. I particularly like the combination of a firm white fish, such as monkfish, and delicate mussels. You will need to use a good stock to bring out the flavour of the fish.

Heat the **Flora Oil** in a large non-stick flame-proof casserole. When it is hot, add the onion and cook for 1 minute. Add the garlic, thyme, fennel and bay leaf and continue to cook, stirring occasionally, until the onion is soft and translucent.

Pour in the fish stock and bring to the boil. Add the mussels and cod. Cover and cook for about 5 minutes, until the mussels open. Discard any that remain closed.

Add the prawns and olives and simmer gently for a further 3 minutes.

Meanwhile, in a food processor or liquidizer, blend the pepper with the passata, chilli and basil until smooth. Add this mixture to the fish stew and bring to a simmer. Season to taste with black pepper and serve with crusty bread and salad.

CHICKEN FAJITAS

Servings: 4

Preparation time
30 minutes

Cooking time
6 minutes

INGREDIENTS

- 4 boneless chicken breasts, skin removed
- pinch of sugar • zest and juice of 1 lime
- 1 tbsp **Flora Oil** • 25g (1oz) **Flora Original**

Tomato and Avocado Salsa:

- 4 large tomatoes, de-seeded and finely diced
- ½ tsp chopped red chilli (optional) • juice of 1 lime • 1 small red onion, finely chopped
- 2 medium avocados, peeled, stoned and finely diced • 8 tbsp finely chopped fresh coriander

To serve: 4–8 medium flour tortillas, warmed

A good dish to have with friends – place the ingredients on plates in the centre of the table and let people help themselves and roll their own.

Cut each chicken breast lengthways into 6 thin strips of 1cm. Place in a bowl and stir in the sugar, lime juice and zest and **Flora Oil**. Cover and leave to marinate in the refrigerator for 1–2 hours or, if possible, overnight.

Meanwhile, make the salsa by placing all the ingredients in a large bowl and stirring gently to combine.

Heat the **Flora Original** in a non-stick frying pan. Add the drained chicken pieces and cook for 5–6 minutes, stirring occasionally, until the chicken is cooked through. With a slotted spoon remove the chicken and drain on paper towel to remove excess fat. Set aside.

Sprinkle each tortilla with shredded lettuce, then spread with some of the tomato and avocado salsa, add the chicken pieces and top with a dollop of yoghurt. Roll or fold over and serve immediately.

GARLIC CHICKEN CASSEROLE

Servings: 4

Preparation time
10 minutes

Cooking time
50 minutes

INGREDIENTS

• 2 tbsp **Flora Oil**
• 8 boneless chicken thighs, skinned • 8–10 garlic cloves, peeled
• 2 tbsp sherry vinegar
• 150ml (¼ pt) dry white wine • 250ml (9fl oz) chicken stock • 1 tbsp honey, or to taste • 1 tbsp half-fat crème fraîche (optional) • 1 tbsp chopped fresh flat-leaf parsley
To serve: steamed broccoli and jacket potatoes

A one-pot dish that is easy to cook and full of flavour and protein. Any left-over chicken can be used the next day in a salad or simply re-heated.

Preheat oven to 180°C/350°F/Gas 4.

Heat the **Flora Oil** in a flameproof casserole, add the chicken and cook for 8–10 minutes, turning occasionally, until brown all over. Set aside.

Cook the garlic cloves in the same pan until softened and golden. Add the sherry vinegar, white wine and chicken stock, then add the chicken and its juices.

Place the casserole, covered, in the oven, and cook for 30 minutes. With a slotted spoon, remove the chicken and keep warm. Tip the remaining contents of the casserole into a food processor or blender and purée until smooth. Return the mixture to the casserole, bring to the boil and bubble rapidly until reduced and slightly thickened. Stir in honey to taste; for a special finish, add a tablespoon of half-fat crème fraîche.

Pour the sauce over the chicken, sprinkle with parsley. Serve with hot vegetables.

VEGETABLE TAGINE

Servings: 4

Preparation time
25 minutes

Cooking time
40 minutes

INGREDIENTS

• 1 tbsp **Flora Oil** • 1 large onion, chopped • 2 garlic cloves, crushed • 1 tsp ground ginger • 1 tsp freshly ground black pepper • 1 tsp ground cinnamon • 85g (3oz) ready-to-eat dried apricots • 25g (1oz) sultanas or raisins • 1 tbsp tomato purée • 425ml (¾pt) vegetable stock • 1 medium sweet potato, peeled and cut into chunks • 1 green pepper, de-seeded and cut into chunks • 1 small aubergine, cut into chunks • 400g can chickpeas, drained and rinsed • 400g can chopped tomatoes • 175g (6oz) cauliflower florets • 175g (6oz) frozen peas • handful of chopped fresh coriander • freshly cooked couscous

You can add your own favourite vegetables to this dish, but remember to add first the ones that take the longest time to cook. The spices increase the intensity of the flavour.

Heat the **Flora Oil** in a large flame-proof casserole. Add the onion, garlic and spices and cook gently, stirring occasionally, until softened but not browned.

Add the apricots, sultanas, tomato purée and stock. Bring to the boil, reduce the heat and simmer until the sauce has reduced by half.

Stir in the sweet potato, green pepper, aubergine, chickpeas and tomatoes. Cover and simmer gently for 10 minutes.

Stir in the cauliflower, cover and simmer gently for 5 minutes. Add the peas, cover and continue to simmer gently for about 10 minutes or until all the vegetables are tender.

Sprinkle with the coriander and serve with couscous.

PORK, PRUNE AND APPLE HOT POT

Servings: 4

Preparation time
20 minutes

Cooking time
1 ¼ hours

INGREDIENTS

• 4 lean pork chops, each about 175g (6oz) • 85g (3oz) prunes, stones removed • 1 small cooking apple, peeled, cored and sliced • 450g (1lb) potatoes, thinly sliced • 1 medium onion, chopped • 25g (1oz) **Flora Original** • freshly ground black pepper • 1 bay leaf • 500ml (18fl oz) chicken stock **To serve:** freshly cooked carrot and courgette ribbons

This is a quick and simple one-pot supper dish. The potatoes soak up all the cooking juices in the dish and develop a great flavour. For a more intense apple flavour, substitute dry cider for half the stock.

Preheat oven to 180°C/350°F/Gas 4.

Put the chops in a casserole and add the prunes. Arrange the apples, potatoes and onion over the top and dot with the **Flora Original**. Season with pepper, add the bay leaf and pour the stock over the chops.

Cover and cook in the oven for 1 hour. Remove the lid and continue cooking for about 15 minutes or until the top has browned. Serve with the vegetables.

FRUIT FOOL

Servings: 4

Preparation time
10 minutes

Cooking time
10 minutes

INGREDIENTS

• 450g (1lb) prepared fruit, such as rhubarb, apricots, peaches or plums, cut into small chunks • 4 tbsp orange juice • 55g (2oz) demerara sugar, or to taste • grated zest of 1 orange • 1 tbsp elder-flower cordial (optional) • 300ml (½pt) ready-made low-fat custard • 125ml (¼pt) low-fat Greek yoghurt

To serve: orange zest and biscuits

The combination of fruit and custard is hard to resist in this recipe, which is surprisingly light and is loved by kids and adults alike. Depending on the sweetness of the fruit you use, you may find that you do not need to add sugar.

Put the fruit into a saucepan and add the orange juice, demerara sugar, orange zest and elderflower cordial, if using. Bring just to the boil, cover and simmer gently, stirring occasionally, until the fruit is soft. Allow the mixture to cool.

Pour the mixture into a food processor or blender, add the custard and process. Add the yoghurt and process until smooth.

Pour the mixture into chilled glasses and keep in the refrigerator until required. Decorate with orange zest and biscuits.

BAKED AMARETTI PEACHES

Servings: 6

Preparation time
5 minutes

Cooking time
25 minutes

INGREDIENTS

• 6 large ripe peaches; alternatively, canned peaches, but choose ones canned in natural fruit juice • ½ packet amaretti biscuits • 25g (1oz) flaked almonds, toasted • ½ tsp ground ginger • 55g (2oz) **Flora Original** • 2–3 tbsp orange juice

A wonderful Italian dessert, giving a slight almond flavour thanks to the amaretti biscuits. You can add a splash of vin santo (sweet sherry) while the peaches are cooking to give the dish an extra kick.

Preheat oven to 375°F/190°C/Gas 5.

Make a small criss-cross pattern at the end of each peach. Bring a saucepan of water to the boil. Drop the peaches into the boiling water and then remove with a slotted spoon and put into a bowl of ice-cold water; the skins should slip off easily. If not, repeat the process. Cut the peaches in half and remove the stones.

Arrange the peach halves, cut side up.

Put the amaretti biscuits, almonds and ginger in a food processor and process until crumbled. Add the **Flora Original** and process to make a paste.

Spoon the mixture into the centres of the peach halves. Pour the orange juice over the peaches and bake for 25 minutes, until they are soft and golden, occasionally basting with the orange juice while they are cooking.

HONEY, ORANGE AND THYME BRAN MUFFINS

Servings: makes 12

Preparation time
15 minutes

Cooking time
20 minutes

INGREDIENTS

• 225g (8oz) self-raising flour • ½ tsp baking powder • 115g (4oz) oat bran • 55g (2oz) light soft brown sugar • 2 tbsp runny honey • 85g (3oz) **Flora Original** • finely grated rind of 2 oranges • ½ tsp fresh thyme leaves • 2 medium eggs • 150ml (¼ pt) butter-milk or natural low-fat yoghurt •150ml (¼ pt) skimmed milk

A delicious muffin that tastes great. Good for breakfast or as a snack.

Preheat oven to 200°C/400°F/Gas 6.

Sieve the flour and baking powder into a large bowl, add the remaining ingredients and mix well. Spoon the mixture into 12 greased muffin tins.

Bake in the oven for 20–25 minutes. The muffins are best served warm.

Alternatives

You can use this recipe as a basis for muffins with different flavours.

For savoury muffins omit the sugar, honey and orange rind and add savoury ingredients; for example, use 1 large grated courgette plus 55g (2oz) diced lean ham and sprinkle with a little finely grated mature Cheddar before putting the muffins in the oven.